A Path Beyond Suffering

Working the Buddhist Method

A Path Beyond Suffering:

Working the Buddhist Method

©2008, John G. Cunyus,
All Rights Reserved

No portion of this work may be copied in any manner whatsoever without written permission from the author, except in the case of brief quotations embodied in critical articles or reviews.

Searchlight Press
Who Are You Looking For?
5634 Ledgestone Drive
Dallas, Texas 75214-2026 USA
888-896-6081
ISBN 10: 0-9644609-6-3
ISBN 13: 978-0-9644609-6-6

Manufactured in the United States of America

ut iterum fluant

– Ecclesiastes i.vii.

Life, as many of us experience it, is full of suffering. Suffering arises from desire. We manage suffering only to the extent we manage desire: overcome desire and overcome suffering as well.

Buddhism offers a time-tested, accessible method for overcoming suffering. Though some are interested in Buddhism as a philosophy or a religion, I am interested in it as a sufferer.

As such, my purpose in writing is not to convert you to a new religion or to put down your old one. It is to help us deal with pain and live more fully. In that spirit, I invite you to share this ancient method that still seems fresh and new.

John Cunyus
Dallas, Texas
2008

If you would like to get in touch with me, please do so at: John@JohnCunyus.com.

Please visit my website, www.JohnCunyus.com, and my blog, http://blog.myspace.com/johncunyus.

Table of Contents

**Why Would a Christian Minister
Write a Book about Buddhism . . .** 8

An Introduction to Buddhism 14
    A Key Text
    Overview
    Beliefs
    Later Developments
    What Is the Buddhist Method?
    Meditation: What It Is and How to Do It
    Simple Meditation Exercises

The Method in Outline 30
    The Four Noble Truths
    The Eightfold Path
    The Ten Perfections
    The Five Skandhas
    Three Elements of Buddhist Practice
    The Five Precepts
    Five Buddhist Precepts, Slightly Updated
    The Wheel of Existence
    Death from a Buddhist Perspective
    How Long Is a World Cycle
    Three Marks of Existence
    Four Attachments
    What Is Wisdom
    The Advantage of Wisdom
    The Advantage of Meditation
    How to Develop Spiritual Power
    The Four Trances

The Four Sublime States
A Meditation on Beauty
A Meditation on Death
The Four Intent Contemplations
Confidence in the Doctrine
Proper Motivation for Teaching the Method
A Refuge in a World of Constant Change
Five Nots
The Danger of Belief
Summary of the Human Condition

Deeper Reflections   **64**
Life Hurts
A Non-Personal Understanding of Life
A Meditation on the Three Marks of Existence
What Is *Nirvana*
A Willingness to Face Death
Indian Psychology
Ten Perfections of a Bodhisattva
A Radical Negation
Why Do Bad Things Happen, Period
Salvation in Hindu and Buddhist Thought
God in Buddhism
What in Tarnation Is Reincarnation?

Applications   **116**
Five Steps to a Happier Life
Five Ways Our Thoughts Can Make Us Sick
Even Gandhi Had Karma
Death on the Wheel of Existence
How to Use the Skandhas for Peace of Mind
The Anger-Eating Demon

Miscellaneous **138**
    Bibliography
    About the Author
    Also by the Author
    Readers Say
    Special Thanks

Why Would a Christian Minister Write a Book About the Buddhist Method . . .

. . . and why would another Christian want to read it?

I have been asked many questions related to my personal faith since I left parish ministry in 2005. I want to note before I answer any of them the depth of concern it takes to ask such questions. Most of us shy away from discussing issues of faith, for fear of offending or out of wariness. Yet we might be too reserved, at times.

If someone you cared about were inside a burning house and you had the opportunity to save them, wouldn't you risk making an effort? If asking someone else about his or her faith might help that person escape hell or death, isn't it worth the risk of rejection? If your soul was in jeopardy and hell loomed before you, wouldn't you want someone to tell you?

Perhaps my house of faith is burning and someone's question may wake me to my danger. If I have fallen away, perhaps I can be reclaimed. One friend, having read my blog entries and received a draft copy of this book, asked straight out if I had "abandoned our Lord and Savior, Jesus Christ, for other religions?"

Is that what studying Buddha's method means?

No, it does not. I confessed Christ as Lord and was baptized on Thursday, March 30, 1972. I was born again a few years later. I was ordained as a Christian minister May 29, 1988, some twenty years and a day prior to writing these words.

I couldn't deny those things, even if I wanted to. I knew both when I accepted Christ as my Lord and when I accepted ordination as His minister that those doors opened only one direction. I cannot turn back.

What changed, then?

I tried for many years to look at life only through the lenses of the Christian tradition. I began to study other traditions during my years at college only with great anxiety. Many times, those who didn't grow up under the influence of Bible-Belt Protestantism don't really appreciate what a struggle it is for those who did to look beyond specifically Christian teachings.

Throughout my professional ministry, I was bound by ordination promises to uphold and proclaim within the Christian tradition exclusively. When that phase of my life crashed to a close, I found again the comfort of the Wisdom tradition. In the Bible, the Wisdom tradition includes all or part of several books: Job, Psalms, Proverbs, and

Ecclesiastes in the Old Testament, as well as much of the New Testament.

I understand Jesus Christ primarily through the lenses of the Wisdom tradition. Most Christian practice focuses on devotion, rather than wisdom. Christians are devoted to a Savior who redeems them personally from sin and death. We believe we are redeemed from such things and, for the most part, stop there.

The Wisdom tradition, however, goes deeper. Since all of us will die, without exception, Wisdom focuses on something other than avoiding the unavoidable. It focuses on living a meaningful life, here and now. Words attributed to King Solomon from Proverbs 1:33 point out Wisdom's effect in a nutshell: " . . . *he who listens to me [Wisdom] will dwell secure and will be at ease, without dread of evil.*"

Needless to say, most people want exactly that. The Wisdom tradition takes that beyond a mere longing and shows us how to accomplish it in life. Though no one does it perfectly, those who walk with Wisdom find a measure of peace most folks do not.

Christian theology affirms that the One we are devoted to, the Savior, is also the source of Wisdom. We need not choose between Wisdom and devotion, because Jesus Christ embodies

perfect Wisdom. The Gospel of John, for instance, begins with a hymn of praise to *Logos*, a word taken from Greek Wisdom traditions and applied directly to Jesus:
> *In the beginning was the word (Logos, in Greek), and the word was with God, and the word was God.*

In "O Come, O Come, Emmanuel," an ancient Latin hymn still sung near Christmas, we sing
> *O come, Thou wisdom from on high,*
> *And order all things far and nigh.*

Buddhism, as I describe it in this book, is a Wisdom tradition. As such, it stands in a similar relationship to Jesus Christ, the *Logos* of God, as any other such Wisdom tradition, including those of the Hebrews and Greeks. If the wisdom in it is genuine, it reflects the only Wisdom there is.

What makes a Wisdom tradition valid? The proof, for me, must come in the living, not in the disputing. As Jesus put it in John 8:32, "... *you will know the truth, and the truth will make you free.*" Does the tradition we are studying help us live in ways that do not violate fundamental Christian principles? Basic Buddhist principles like honesty, self-discipline, nonviolence, and compassion violate nothing I know of in Christianity.

One question we should ask when we consider an "alien" Wisdom tradition like Buddhism, is whether Wisdom has to belong only to one tradition to be valid? Does the name brand matter, once we get beyond the packaging? Is truth true, regardless of where we find it? Could it be, as Jesus said in Matthew 11:19, that *"wisdom is justified by her deeds."*

If so, we can say that Gautama, the Buddha, taught Christ, in the sense that he taught a powerful, transcendent Wisdom. The Wisdom he taught *makes us free* in the sense that it brings us to a place beyond selfishness, beyond the normal fixation with the things of this life. Buddha never tells us who or what it is we encounter in that place, referring to it only as *Nirvana*. He stresses what the Ultimate is not, rather than what it is.

Yet in that place where his method leads, we encounter a *peace that passes all understanding,*[1] remarkably like what Christians find in Christ. Could it be that Christian revelation makes explicit what remains implicit in the Buddhist method, much as many Christians believe the Gospel completes the faith of the Old Testament? If so, shouldn't we celebrate the Buddhist method, rather than condemn it?

---

[1] See Philippians 4:7.

My hope is that we have hearts courageous enough to seek truth wherever it may be found. I am convinced that, wherever we find gentle spirits, living in peace, building others up, living a Wisdom that leads beyond suffering, we find Christ – regardless of the name being used.

That's how a Christian minister could write a book like this, and why another Christian might want to read it.

An Introduction to Buddhism

Key Text

We are what we think.
All that we are arises
with our thoughts.
With our thoughts
we make the world.
Speak or act
with an impure mind
and trouble will follow you
as the wheel
follows the ox
that draws the cart.

We are what we think.
All that we are
arises with our thoughts.
With our thoughts
we make the world.
Speak or act
with a pure mind
and happiness
will follow you
as your shadow,
unshakable.

(Siddhartha Gautama, the Buddha,
from The Dhammapada)

Overview

Buddhism was born in India some 600 years before Christ. Its founder, Siddhartha Gautama, was the eldest son of a Nepalese king. Gautama, having grasped the reality of suffering, abandoned the world at the age of 29 in order to seek enlightenment. Gautama spent six years studying with various Hindu religious leaders and practicing severe austerities. At the end of this period, he relaxed his self-torturing discipline and attained *Nirvana* under a tree in Bodh Gaya, in what is now India.

Buddha likened Nirvana, the Ultimate, to a fire which has burned itself out. In *Nirvana* all clinging to individuality, and with it all suffering, ceases. Buddha's method approached *Nirvana* negatively, defining what it is not. It is not that *Nirvana* is unreal or imaginary. It is that human words are not capable of expressing it by anything other than analogy. In Buddha's thought, many of us get so caught up in the language we use to describe the Ultimate that we lose sight of the reality all together. Thus Buddhism largely dispenses with positive descriptions of *Nirvana*.

During his lifetime, Gautama, now called the Buddha, meaning "awakened one," traveled widely winning converts. In doing so, he established the oldest, continuously-enduring human institution,

Buddhist monasticism. Following his death at age 80, his movement expanded throughout Southeast Asia, before moving north into China, Korea, Japan, and Tibet. Displaced from its south Asian home by the Muslim invasions beginning in the 7th Century AD, Buddhism continued to thrive outside the borders of its native land.

There are three major divisions of Buddhism. Theravada Buddhism, similar in tone and practice to the original teachings of the Buddha himself, continues to be practiced in Sri Lanka and in the countries of Southeast Asia. Mahayana Buddhism is the predominant form in China, Korea, and Japan. Tantric Buddhism, a third variant, combines elements of both prior traditions. It is practiced in Tibet, as well as elsewhere.

Original Buddhism did not regard the Buddha as a god. The Buddha's teaching strictly avoided metaphysical questions, considering such questions useless for breaking the cycle of human suffering. Buddhism insists that the individual self as we commonly understand it is an illusion. The effect of Buddhist practice is to enable one to escape from that illusion and the suffering it brings.

Beliefs

Buddhism styles itself as "The Middle Way," the rational middle ground between self-denial and self-indulgence. Original Buddhism was simple and austere, easily taught and easily grasped – even if difficult to realize in practice.

Four Noble Truths
Gautama's Four Noble Truths outline the essence of the Buddhist world view.
> 1. Suffering. Life as we know it is full of suffering and frustration.
> 2. The Origin of Suffering. The origin of suffering is desire – to have what we do not have and not to have what we do have.
> 3. The Cessation of Suffering. Suffering ends when we cut the root of desire.
> 4. The Eightfold Path to the Cessation of Suffering. (Outlined below)

The Eightfold Path
Gautama's Eightfold Path provided a blueprint for escaping the inevitable suffering of the world. The elements of the path are:
> 1. Right Views, seeing the world as it is, devoid of Ego.
> 2. Right Intentions, including the intention to do no harm.
> 3. Right Speech, avoiding speech that deceives or degrades another.

4. Right Action, living respectfully of life and those with whom we share it.
5. Right Livelihood, work which does not harm another.
6. Right Effort, to quell passion and attachment.
7. Right Mindfulness, being aware of what is happening in the present moment.
8. Right Concentration, meditating on truths which lead us to *Nirvana*.

MONASTICISM

Like the other significant Indian religious movements of its day, original Buddhism believed that true liberation, *Nirvana*, was available only to a few. These few formed the *sangha*, the monastic community of those who had left the world in order to put Buddhism into practice. Salvation was nearly impossible for lay believers, whose religious duty was to support the monks in their efforts. Becoming a monk involved surrendering all one's possessions, begging for a living, and living apart from the ordinary world.

REINCARNATION

Like Hinduism, Buddhism shares the concept of reincarnation. Though in Buddhist thought there is no real self to be born again, there are actions, karma, which carry over from one lifetime to another. By accepting the Buddha's teaching and putting it into practice, one can move closer to the point when *Nirvana* is attained. Like a blown-out candle flame, at that moment all clinging to individuality, and with it all suffering, ceases.

Later Developments

Original Buddhism focused on liberating individuals from the eternal round of sorrow. Siddhartha Gautama was a man, not a god. What remained after his death was simply his teaching, the *dharma*, which was sufficient to guide the sincere to liberation.

Mahayana Buddhism rejected this vision as too narrow and selfish. It was not enough to liberate oneself, the Mahayana taught. The goal must be the liberation of all beings. Mahayana Buddhism held up as its ideal not the individual saint of original Buddhism, but the *Bodhisattva*, the "being of truth," who vowed not to enter final enlightenment until all beings had entered it.

Mahayana Buddhism also developed a new understanding of the Buddha himself. While Siddhartha Gautama was the historical Buddha, the Buddha nature itself pervaded the universe. Innumerable individuals, past and future, had realized this Buddha nature. Those who in this world called on the name of the Buddhas and *Bodhisattvas* could expect to be reborn in places more congenial to enlightenment.

Tantric Buddhism integrated magical and mystical practices into the life of the religion. Taking deep root in isolated Tibet, Tantric Buddhism remained largely unknown to the outside world until the Chinese takeover of that country forced many of its religious leaders into exile.

Buddhism today has spread beyond Asia into Europe and North America, carried by Asian immigrants and philosophically-minded Westerners. After Christianity and Islam, Buddhism is the world's third great missionary religion.

What Is the "Buddhist Method?"

The Buddhist method has three basic elements: Wisdom, Morality, and Meditation. All weigh more or less equally in daily living.

Wisdom is more than mere knowledge. Wisdom understands the way the universe works. It works with the flow of existence, not against it. Wisdom," as Jesus said in the Gospel of Matthew, "is known by all her children." The Buddhist method centers on the search for and the application of wisdom.

Morality is common to all people, everywhere. "That which is hateful to you," Rabbi Hillel reportedly said in the 1st Century of the Common Era, "do to no one. This is the law and the prophets." The Buddhist method teaches a practical morality, because it understands that to hurt another is to hurt ourselves.

Meditation is the internal practice of the Buddhist method. Meditation can take the form of active reflection on the insights of the wise. In this regard, Christian practices like mental prayer and *lectio divina*, the prayerful reading of sacred texts, are forms of meditation. Meditation can also be purely contemplative, quieting the mind and focusing on the present. There is no Buddhist method without meditation.

The method is all these together. Those who understand it only as a wisdom tradition, an ethical teaching, as a religion, or an academic pursuit, do not understand it at all. We must put the method into practice through meditation for it to work.

By combining wisdom, morality, and meditation, we discover the benefit in the method. Like the prescriptions of any good doctor, Gautama's prescriptions only work if followed.

Meditation
    (What It Is and How to Do It)

Yes, you can take courses and spend lots of money learning. To tell the truth, though, meditation isn't all that complicated. The basic techniques are straightforward. As is so often true in life, the problem lies not in knowing how to do something. The problem lies in actually doing it. Meditation begins with breathing. If we can breathe, we can meditate.

Most times, we are unaware of our breath, just as we are unaware of most of what goes on around us in the rush of our daily lives. We only become aware of what is happening to us in the present moment when something reaches up into our conscious mind and grabs our attention: pain, for instance, or danger.

Because we are unaware of what actually takes place around us, we find ourselves swept along on a torrent of thought, emotion, worry, and stress. We have no perspective on our daily troubles, no sense of existing apart from them. Do you ever feel like you've been snagged on a spinning wheel, with no apparent way off?

Meditation helps us get off the wheel, if only for a moment. When we meditate, we relax physically and mentally. Our stress levels decrease. We recover a bit of perspective. For me, those things are valuable enough to make me take meditation seriously.

So, how do you meditate? One of the simplest techniques is simply to count your breaths. Sit down comfortably, with your back and neck relatively straight. Let yourself become aware of your entire body. Close your eyes gently. Hear all the sounds around you.

Then bring your attention to your breathing. Do nothing more or less than count your breaths. When you catch your mind wandering, just bring it back to the task at hand.

For beginners, start your meditation by counting thirty breaths. Some teachers suggest we begin with more, but sometimes the larger number becomes a stress in itself. In my meditation experience, I've found that counting fewer than thirty doesn't really give me time to settle in. Thirty is a nice starting point. Of course, you can do more or less if you choose.

Your mind will wander as you meditate. That's neither good nor bad, since that's just what your mind does. The difference between meditation and ordinary awareness is that in meditation you bring your awareness back to the breath when your mind wanders. In ordinary awareness, you let your mind go where it will.

You don't have to sit in exotic yoga postures to

meditate. It would be nice if we all could, but most of us aren't that limber. Just sit comfortably.

Meditation is not a religious act, in and of itself. From a physiological standpoint, you are doing nothing more or less than triggering the "relaxation response" in your brain, something that is well-documented in scientific literature. This relaxation response has positive benefits, regardless of your religious orientation.

There isn't a "right way" and a "wrong way" to do it. Much of the value in meditation comes from the things that cross our awareness as we meditate. We may find our mind spinning as we begin our meditation. There may be no sense of peace or perspective. When we finish, though, we know more about what's really going on in our lives than we did before we started. There is a value in that.

So, give it a try. Take a breath. Hear the world around you. Count your breaths. See where it leads.

All you have to lose is a little stress.

Simple Meditation Exercises

1. Sit very still. Count your breaths to 30. When your mind wanders, bring it back.

2. Sit very still. Count your thoughts to 30. When your mind wanders, bring it back.

3. Set a timer for 10 minutes. Sit very still. Be aware of every sensation in your body, every thought in your mind, without holding on to any of them. When your mind wanders, bring it back.

4. Sit very still. Repeat 30 times to yourself one of the lists in the Buddhism in Outline section below (such as The Four Noble Truths, The Ten Perfections, or the like). Say each word slowly, in the same tempo as your breath. Keep the word at the center of your awareness for the length of each breath. When your mind wanders, bring it back.

5. Set a timer for 30 minutes. Read slowly, focusing on the meaning of every word, one of the chapters in a holy book.

Write down the thoughts, emotions, and sensations you experience. Summarize. Then, in a week, revisit what you wrote.

At the end of each meditation, reflect on what you experienced.

****

> "Be a warrior, Arjuna,
> and kill desire,
> great enemy of the soul."
>
> – *Bhagavad-Gita, 3:42.*

****

Buddhism in Outline

Four Noble Truths
> (The Four Noble Truths are the heart of the Buddhist method.)

1. Suffering
Life as we know it is full of suffering and frustration.

2. Origin of Suffering
The origin of suffering is desire – to have what we do not have and not to have what we do have.

3. Overcoming of Suffering
Suffering ends when we cut the root of desire.

4. The Eightfold Path to the Cessation of Suffering
- Right View
- Right Intention
- Right Speech
- Right Action
- Right Livelihood
- Right Effort
- Right Mindfulness
- Right Concentration

(Outlined in detail below.)

****

The Eightfold Path
>(The Eightfold Path leads us systematically beyond suffering.)

1. Right View
Right View entails seeing the world as it is, devoid of a permanent ego.

2. Right Intention
Right Intention intends no harm.

3. Right Speech
Right Speech means avoiding speech that deceives or degrades.

4. Right Action
Right Action involves living respectfully of life and those with whom we share it.

5. Right Livelihood
Right Livelihood involves earning our living in a way that does not harm living things.

6. Right Effort
Right Effort seeks to quell passion and surrender attachment.

7. Right Mindfulness
Right Mindfulness practices being aware of what is happening in the present moment.

8. Right Concentration
Right Concentration involves ongoing meditation on the truths which open our awareness of *Nirvana*.

****

The Ten Perfections

(The Ten Perfections are the ideals which guide us on the path. The analogies come from ancient accounts.)

1. Generosity
The generosity of those walking the path of the perfections is compared to a glass of water that has been overturned. It gives all, unconditionally.

2. Precepts
According to an ancient story, a yak would rather die than allow its beautiful tail to be torn. We would rather give up our lives than violate the precepts[2].

3. Renunciation
Long-held hostages long only for the moment of release. So we renounce any nostalgia for those things that imprison us.

4. Wisdom
A beggar begs from all, without distinction. Some of the most unlikely passersby prove the most generous. We beg wisdom from all, not judging on the basis of exteriors.

---

[2] 1. Respect life. 2. Respect property. 3. Respect promises. 4. Respect words. 5. Respect the body.

5. Courage
Lions are always courageous, whatever they face. So we live courageously, braving all for the sake of the path.

6. Patience
The earth does not turn away from anything dumped on it[3]. Neither do we as we walk the path.

7. Truth
The morning star never varies from its course through the sky. We, too, move in accordance with truth.

8. Determination
As mountain peaks stand firm in all weather, so we face whatever comes, unwilling to be moved from what we have resolved to do.

9. Good Will
Water cleanses and refreshes all, regardless of moral qualification. So we treat all living things with equal good will.

10. Indifference

---

[3] This does not mean there are no consequences when something is dumped out, only that no selfish objection is raised.

Earth is not concerned for its own gain, whatever those who live on its surface do[4]. So we give up all concern for personal gain or loss.

****

---

[4] Again, this does not imply approval of all that is done on earth's surface, only the absence of a self-centered response.

The Five Skandhas
>(Buddha taught that human experience can be understood as the interplay of five impersonal elements, called *skandhas*.)

1. Form
I carve a statue out of a hunk of marble. The finished product is a form. That is the **skandha of form.**

2. Sensation
The statue is able to feel. That is the **skandha of sensation.**

3. Preference
The statue likes certain feelings and dislikes others. That is the **skandha of preference.**

4. Conditioning
The statue over time learns to expect certain sensations from certain actions. That is the **skandha of conditioning.**

5. Consciousness
By connecting forms, sensations, preferences, and conditioning, the statue develops a sense of an ongoing awareness. That is the **skandha of consciousness.**

****

Three Elements of Buddhist Practice
(These three elements summarize the Buddhist method of overcoming suffering.)

1. Wisdom
Wisdom is the unchanging truth of the universe. It is open to those who approach it humbly, with their passions under control.

2. Morality
Morality enables us to live without harming either others or ourselves.

3. Meditation
Meditation is the mental practice of the Buddhist method. Through meditation, the method comes alive in us.

****

The Five Precepts
(These five precepts are binding on all Buddhists, lay and monastic alike.)

1. Respect life.
Traditionally, "Do not take life."

2. Respect property.
Traditionally, "Do not steal."

3. Respect promises.
Traditionally, "Do not commit sexual immorality."

4. Respect words.
Traditionally, "Do not speak harmfully or untruthfully."

5. Respect bodies.
Traditionally, "Do not use intoxicants."

****

Five Buddhist Precepts, Slightly Updated

1. Refrain from taking life. What we cannot create, we ought not destroy.

2. Watch what you say. Hurtful words, hateful words, and untrue words set the world on fire. We would be better off saying nothing than saying such things.

3. Sex is a wonderful thing, so treat it with respect. Respect not only the act, but those with whom you have it.

4. Don't take what isn't yours. Jesus Christ's Golden Rule, "Do unto others as you would have them do unto you" sums up Buddhist ethics as well, as long as we expand it to apply to all living things.

5. Watch what you put into your body. Some substances and some attitudes are clearly toxic, both to ourselves and to those around us. Know when to say, "Thanks, but no thanks," even to yourself.

****

The Wheel of Existence
(The Wheel of Existence explains the mechanism of suffering.)

From uncertainty, change arises;
From change, consciousness arises;
From consciousness, the world outside arises;
From the world outside, the senses arise;
From the senses, contact arises;
From contact, sensation arises;
From sensation, desire arises;
From desire, attachment arises;
From attachment, existence arises;
From existence, birth arises;
From birth, old age and death, sorrow, lamentation, misery, grief, and despair arise.

Thus this entire aggregation of misery arises.

When uncertainty fades out and ceases, change comes to an end;
When change ceases, consciousness comes to an end;
When consciousness ceases, the world outside comes to an end;
When the world outside ceases, the senses come to an end;
When the senses cease, contact comes to an end;
When contact ceases, sensation comes to an end;
When sensation ceases, desire comes to an end;
When desire ceases, attachment comes to an end;

When attachment ceases, existence comes to an end;
When existence ceases, birth comes to an end;
When birth ceases, old age and death, sorrow, lamentation, misery, grief and despair come to an end as well.

Thus this entire aggregation of misery ceases.

****

Death, from a Buddhist Perspective

"For when, in any existence, one arrives at the gate of death, either in the natural course of things or through violence; and when, by a concourse of intolerable, death-dealing pains, all the members *(of the body)*, both great and small, are loosened and wrenched apart . . .; and the body, like a green palm-leaf exposed to the sun, dries up by degrees; and eye-sight and the other senses fail; and the power of feeling, and the power of thinking, and vitality are making the last stand in the heart – then consciousness residing in that last refuge, the heart, continues to exist by virtue of . . . predispositions.

[This consciousness] still retains something of what it depends on, and consist of such former deeds as were weighty, much practiced, and are now close at hand; or else, [consciousness] creates a reflex in itself or of the mode of life now being entered upon, and it is with this as its object that consciousness continues to exist.

This consciousness being in its series inclined toward the object of desire, and impelled toward it by predispositions, like a man who swings himself over a ditch by means of a rope hanging from a tree on the hither bank, quits its first resting-place and continues to subsist in dependence on objects of sense and other things . . .

Here the former consciousness, from its passing out of existence, is called passing away, and the latter, from its being reborn into a new existence, is called rebirth."

(<u>Buddhism: In Translations</u>, pgs 238-239, Hereinafter cited as BIT.)

****

How Long Is a World Cycle
(This saying from "*Samyutta-Nikaya*" illustrates the vastness of time, from a Buddhist perspective.)

It is as if, O priest, there were a mountain consisting of a great rock, a league[5] in length, a league in width, a league in height, without break, cleft, or hollow, and every hundred years a man were to come and rub it once with a silken garment; that mountain consisting of a great rock, O priest, would more quickly wear away and come to an end than a world cycle. O priest, this is the length of a world cycle. And many such cycles, O priest, have rolled by, and many hundreds of cycles, and many thousands of cycles, and many hundreds of thousands of cycles. And why do I say so? Because, O priest, this round of existence is without known starting point; and of beings who course and roll along from birth to birth, blinded by ignorance and fettered by desire, there is no beginning discernible."
(BIT, pgs 315-316.)

****

---

[5]A league is three miles

Three Marks of Existence
(We can expect these three marks to be part of all experiences in life.)

1. Impermanence
Life is impermanent. The only constant is change. Our jobs, our relationships, our circumstances, our bodies themselves, all are in perpetual change. Things in the natural world that seem permanent aren't really. The earth lasts longer than we do, yet even its forms pass away over time. Nothing in life endures forever.

2. Dissatisfaction
Dissatisfaction is also a way of life. We are seldom content with things, at least not for long. No matter how much we buy, have, or make, there will always be an unease beneath it.

3. Lack of Ego
What we think of as the ego is a collection of ideas, memories, emotions, sounds, and sights, all clustered around our physical existence. There is no permanent, separate identity behind it.

****

The Four Attachments
(We tend to be attached to four ideas, each of which leads to unnecessary suffering.)

Sensual Desire: Not surprisingly, we only want to experience pleasant sensations. We suffer both when we attain them, because they disappoint us, and when we don't attain them.

Ego: We remain attached to the idea of ourselves as distinct, permanent entities, existing apart from the natural processes of the universe.

False Belief: From a Buddhist perspective, false belief is belief either in a permanent ego or belief in an ego that comes to an end.

Useless Action: If we believe our ego is permanent, we frantically try to save it from destruction. If we do not believe in an enduring ego, we disregard many things in life we ought to be more respectful of. Either extreme represents useless action.

****

What Is Wisdom

"What, O priests, is the discipline of elevated wisdom? Whenever, O priests, a priest knows the truth concerning misery, knows the truth concerning the origin of misery, knows the truth concerning the cessation of misery, knows the truth concerning the path leading to the cessation of misery, this, O priests, is called the discipline in elevated wisdom."
(BIT, pg 330.)

****

The Advantage of Wisdom

"What advantage, O priests, is gained by training in insight? Wisdom is developed. And what advantage is gained by the development of wisdom? Ignorance is abandoned."
(<u>BIT</u>, pg. 330)

****

The Advantage of Meditation

"What advantage, O priests, is gained by training in quiescence? The thoughts are trained. And what advantage is gained by training of the thoughts? Passion is abandoned."
                    (BIT, pg. 288)

****

The Four Trances
(Buddhist meditation induces trance, a state of focused attention. The following describes how the trances are induced and what their characteristics are.)

The First Trance is produced by isolation. It is marked by joy and happiness.

The Second Trance is produced by concentration. Its marks include inner tranquility and insight.

The Third Trance is produced by the fading away of joy. Its marks include indifference, contemplation, and contented living.

The Fourth Trance is produced by the abandonment of both happiness and misery, as well as any past gladness or sorrow. Its marks include a state characterized as "neither happiness nor misery," and by "contemplation refined by indifference."

****

The Four Sublime States
>(We cultivate these four states in all of life's circumstances.)

Friendliness sees all beings and circumstances as teaching us positive lessons on the path.

Compassion means being concerned for the suffering of all beings, even those we normally would not consider.

Joy is the spontaneous feeling of delight we find in meditation.

Indifference no longer judges the world by how it affects us personally.

****

How to Develop Spiritual Power

"If a priest, O priests, should frame a wish . . . then must he be perfect in the precepts, bring his thoughts to a state of quiescence, practice diligently the trances, attain to insight, and be a frequenter of lonely places."
  (BIT, pgs 303-304)

****

A Meditation on Beauty

(This meditation is designed to help us move beyond our obsession with outward appearances.)

". . . nails, teeth, skin, flesh, sinews, bones, marrow of the bones, kidneys, heart, liver, pleura, spleen, lungs, intestines, mesentery, stomach, feces, bile, phlegm, pus, blood, sweat, fat, tears, lymph, saliva, snot, synovial fluid, urine, brain."
(BIT, pg. 130)

****

A Meditation on Death
> (This meditation helps us break the false belief that we will escape death.)

But again, O priests, a priest, if perchance he sees in a cemetery a decaying body one day dead, or two days dead, or three days dead, swollen, black, and full of festering putridity, he compares his own body, saying, 'Verily, my body also has this nature, this destiny, and is not exempt.'
>(BIT, pg. 360-361)

****

The Four Intent Contemplations

(By practicing these four meditations, Buddhists through two millennia have reached the Trance of Cessation, the point at which we touch *Nirvana* in the body.)

1. Breath. We maintain our attention on the breath, letting go of all else. If counting your breaths helps keep you focused, do so.

2. Body. We focus on the entire sensation of the body. Begin with five minutes and work up from there.

3. Mind. Be aware of all the contents of your thought, as if watching from afar.

4. Elements. Focus on a point in your environment. Watch all aspects of what is happening, from a perspective of silence.

As always, when your mind wanders, bring it back.

****

Confidence in the Doctrine
>(This meditation reminds us of the reliability of the method.)

The Doctrine has been well-taught by the Blessed One, avails even in the present life, is immediate in its results, is inviting and conducive to salvation, and may be mastered by any intelligent man for himself.
>(BIT, pg. 419)

****

Proper Motivation for Teaching the Method
(We neither teach nor practice the method for selfish motives.)

". . . and thus teaches the Doctrine to others because of that Doctrine's intrinsic goodness, and because of compassion, mercy, and kindness."
(BIT, pg 419)

****

A Refuge in a World of Constant Change
>(Not clinging to 'I' protects us from additional sorrow.)

>. . . not being possessed with the idea, 'I am form; form belongs to the I,' when form alters and changes, the alteration and change of form do not cause sorrow, lamentation, grief, and despair to rise in him."
>
>>(<u>BIT</u>, pg. 422)

>(The meditation continues by substituting the remaining skandhas for the word "form": sensation, preference, conditioning, and consciousness. This reminds us not to identify ourselves with any aspect of existence.)

****

Five Nots

(This phrase is used as a meditation. Say the words to yourself slowly. Let their meaning seep in. Understand each as an answer to the question, "What am I?")

Not form,
Not sensation,
Not preference,
Not conditioning,
Not consciousness.

****

The Danger of Belief
(Gautama answers a monk, Vaccha, who asks him metaphysical questions. Please note than in documents translated from Pali, Gautama's name is often spelled "Gotama.")

"Does Gotama hold that the world is eternal, and that this view alone is true, and every other false?"

"Nay, Vaccha, I do not hold that the world is eternal, and that this view alone is true, and every other false."

"But how is it, Gotama? Does Gotama hold that the world is not eternal, and that this view alone is true, and every other false?"

"Nay, Vaccha, I do not hold that the world is not eternal, and that this view alone is true, and every other false."

". . . What objection does Gotama perceive to these theories that he has not adopted any of them?"

"Vaccha, the theory that the world is eternal . . . [or that the world is not eternal], is a jungle, a wilderness, a puppet-show, a writhing, and a fetter, and is coupled with misery, ruin, despair, and agony, and does not tend to aversion, absence of passion, cessation, quiescence, knowledge, supreme wisdom, and *Nirvana*."   (BIT, 125-126)

Summary of the Human Condition
>(Taken from "The Summum Bonum," <u>BIT</u>, pgs. 336-347)

Humanity "is captivated, entranced, spellbound by its lusts."

We are "subject to birth, old age, disease, death, sorrow, corruption."

"All . . . partake of these sensual pleasures, and enveloped, besotted, and immersed in them, perceive not their wretchedness, and know not the way of escape."

Realizing our state, we develop "faith, heroism, contemplation, concentration, wisdom."

Through practice of the method, we attain "aversion, absence of passion, quiescence, knowledge, supreme wisdom, and *Nirvana*."

****

****

"Must I fear what others fear?
What nonsense!"

– *Tao Te Ching, Book XX*

****

Deeper Reflections

Life Hurts

Much as we wish it didn't, hard as we try to avoid it, life hurts. It doesn't necessarily hurt all the time, but when it does nothing else seems quite as important. The biggest challenges I have faced in life have all been about dealing with pain of one sort or another.

Pain is the common denominator of human life. It is the common denominator of all life, indeed, not simply the human variety. We don't all believe the same things. Our nationalities differ. Our goals may be complete opposites.

Yet pain is pain, whatever other trappings life brings. There is no such thing as Christian pain, atheist pain, American pain, or Muslim pain. It's just pain. One vital test of any approach to life has to be, "Does it help me deal with pain?"

Too often, the answer surprises us. We pursue some things in life with great gusto, believing them to be important. Consider the way we pursue money, for instance, or beauty.

If we don't have money or beauty, we suffer for it. We suffer not merely because not having money or beauty shuts doors to us in the physical world. We suffer because of what not having money or beauty does to our sense of self. Others may dismiss such suffering, but many of us know full well how much it really hurts.

Any glance at People magazine, though, shows that having money and/or beauty does not exempt us from suffering either. The rich suffer just like the poor. As the Bible puts it, "How the wise man dies, just like the fool."

We may be poor and miserable now. Are we sure we wouldn't just end up rich and miserable if we got what we want? Many people are hell-bent on finding out.

Out of this, though, comes one practical answer for coping with pain. When it comes to wanting things, it doesn't matter if we get what we want or not. The very act of wanting leads to pain. The more we want something, the worse we hurt for it. The opposite statement is also true. The less we want, the less we hurt.

We could make an equation out of it:

More Want=More Hurt
Less Want=Less Hurt

Realizing that leads to certain adjustments. We know that wanting and hurting, desire and pain, go hand-in-hand. Does this mean the way to overcome pain is to not want anything at all? Is the answer being totally passive?

If it is, is that something truly desirable? Aren't some things worth the pain? Most of us would say yes. We all have our list: the well-being of those we love, the principles we hold dear, our communities, large and small, and more.

Wanting the best for our loved ones brings pain at times. Yet, it is a pain we often bear bravely. It's worth it, in other words, under most circumstances. Anyone who has delighted in a child knows this without being told.

Other things, though, turn out not to be worth it, when we weigh the pain they cause against the desire they fulfill. My steak dinner may taste good, for instance. It's a safe bet the cow wouldn't agree it was worth the cost, though.

It may not always be our pain, but some living thing suffers to satisfy just about every desire. We tend to blunder along in life unaware of these things, unfortunately. We tune out pain we don't see.

Let me give an example that goes back to Adam Smith's landmark book, <u>The Wealth of Nations</u>. Let's say I know that 100,000 Chinese will be killed in a natural disaster next week. Most reasonable people would feel sad over that. Few of them outside of China would lose sleep over it, though.

Let's say I also know also that someone in my city will lose a finger in an accident. That seems sad too, though not on the level of what's going to happen in China. I wouldn't likely lose sleep over the impending lost finger, either . . . unless I knew it was mine!

If I know I'm going to lose the finger in the next week, there'll probably be a lot of lost sleep involved! It will bother me far more than the imminent death of 100,000 Chinese. Why is this? **Personal pain moves us far more than abstract pain.**

Still, personal pain is usually what it takes to wake us up to the pain of others. I sometimes dismissed other peoples' suffering, until I suffered myself. Then I understood. Once we know loss, we empathize when others suffer it as well.

We live in a universe of pain and loss. It seems like a good idea to have an effective way of dealing with suffering. That way, we can decide freely what is worth suffering for and what isn't.

For many, the Buddhist method provides such a way. Could it be for us as well? The way to find out by putting it into practice.

****

A Non-Personal Understanding of Life

Ancient Buddhist monks taught that the varied experiences of human life are drawn from five piles, called *skandhas*. Imagine five separate piles of small rocks. Each pile is its own color. As a current takes the rocks and mixes them, they form beautiful, even haunting, patterns.

Yet the patterns constantly change in the current. The patterns resemble objects we recognize at times. We become attached to the patterns, believing fervently in their separate existence.

For all their apparent individuality, though, the patterns are never more than rocks intermingling. The shapes they take, the resemblances, are never permanent.

The five rock piles from which our experience is drawn include

> 1. **Form**: The physical, external aspect of our experience.
>
> 2. **Sensation:** The feeling of living in a body.
>
> 3. **Preference:** Preferring one thing over another.

4. **Conditioning:** The lessons we learn from experience.

5. **Consciousness:** The sense of ourselves as ongoing beings in relationship to the external world.

Ego, the "I" in our experience, arises from this process. Yet no permanent entity corresponding to ego or "I" actually exists. Ego is another pattern in the endless interplay of the skandhas. When the pattern ends, our apparent Ego vanishes as well.

One source of suffering is our false belief in a personal self. Nothing in reality corresponds to our notion of identity. John Cunyus is many things to many different people. Buddhist method teaches that, for all the things he is, he is not a distinct, permanent entity named John Cunyus. When the various elements that constitute him come apart, he will be as extinct as a fire which has been blown out.

His mistaken belief that he is a permanent entity makes him miserable at times. The sense that he is a separate self makes him anxious to protect that self. Yet he tries to protect something that ultimately cannot be protected.

Understanding the skandhas helps John understand what he is and what he isn't. He is an animate body, aware of itself, partly conscious and partly not. He is a series of thoughts, emotions, memories, and sensations. His feelings come and go like clouds in the sky. He can't hold them, even when he wants to.

Human existence seems to be personal, but it isn't. In reality, it is drawn from five great piles, the skandhas. Systematic meditation on the skandhas helps one eliminate the sense of "I," if only for the period of the meditation. This has striking effects, according to those who practice it. Without an "I," nothing in life needs to be taken personally. If "I" am not at risk, "I" don't have to feel threatened.

Those who are able to let go of "I," at least in part, seem to find the path through life a little easier.

****

What Is *Nirvana?*

Buddha likened *Nirvana*, the Ultimate, to a fire which has burned itself out. In *Nirvana* all clinging to individuality, and with it all suffering, ceases. Buddha's method approached *Nirvana* negatively, defining what it is not. It is not that *Nirvana* is unreal or imaginary. It is that human words are not capable of expressing it by anything other than analogy. In Buddha's thought, most humans get so caught up in the language we use to describe the Ultimate that we lose sight of the reality all together. Thus Buddhism largely dispenses with positive descriptions of *Nirvana*.

The timeless peace of *Nirvana* is submerged for almost every living being by a swirl of suffering and frustration. We suffer and become frustrated because of desire. We continually want what we don't have and have what we don't want.

Most of us can't see beyond the "small self" in which our desires imprison us. We believe we are an individual ego, experiencing life "out there," tossed around by the ups and down of daily struggles. We see ourselves as a name, a body, a personal history.

While we cannot put into words what *Nirvana* is, we can say what it isn't. *Nirvana*, the ultimate, isn't a physical form that passes away. It isn't the sensations of physical life, the preferences that arise from them, or the well-worn ruts that those preferences carve in our memories. It isn't even the sense of an ongoing self that these other things engender in the mind.

What is it? Others can point to it, but they can't make us see it. We have to experience it for ourselves, in however limited and halting a fashion. Once we've experienced it, though, we find it easier to live at peace in a world of constant change.

The value in the Buddhist method is that it performs as advertised: practiced religiously, it alleviates suffering. It forces us beyond the confines of the narrow little "I" in which most of us live. It gives us a perspective from which to view the events of our lives dispassionately.

****

A Meditation on the Three Marks of Existence

According to method, existence has three marks: impermanence, dissatisfaction, and egolessness. This isn't a teaching that sits well with modern hearers. Many of us react by condemning Buddha as negative. Life should focus on positive truths, we believe. Yet the teaching is what it is. Why do we react the way we do?

Deep down, in what we imagine to be our "heart of hearts," we wish it weren't true. Many of us would rather pretend life was something different. We partake in the cult of optimism, hoping against hope that someday, somehow, things will be better. However often those hopes are dashed, we would rather keep on believing than come to terms with an unpleasant reality. At least we think of it as unpleasant.

Yet from a brutally honest perspective, Buddha's teaching is right on the nose. Life is impermanent. The only constant is change. Our jobs, our relationships, our circumstances, our bodies themselves, all are in perpetual change. Things in the natural world that seem permanent aren't really. The earth lasts longer than we do, yet even its forms pass away over time. There is nothing in life we can hold on to, a fact that seems bleak and hopeless on the surface.

Dissatisfaction is also a way of life. We are seldom content with things, at least not for long. When we do arrive at a place of contentment, we find it slipping out of our grasp before we even have an opportunity to enjoy it. No matter how much we buy, have, or make, there is always a gnawing unease beneath it. This unease makes the world go around in a sense. Only dissatisfied people keep pushing on to find a better way. Even so, the reality is inescapable.

Egolessness, the Buddhist idea that there is no self, strikes us as the least likely conclusion of the three. After all, most of us have a strong sense of self. We know who we are. We live in a culture that celebrates, even worships, individuality. How can someone say there is no self, no ego?

Buddha tells us that the ego is just an idea. In fact, it is a collection of ideas, memories, emotions, sounds, and sights, all clustered around our physical existence. When we dissect any one of those ideas, memories, and emotions, though, we find the thread unraveling. Am I the 46 year old man now alive or the 17 year old youth of memory? Is "John," my name, anything more than a particular sound associated with particular memories?

One ancient meditation technique strikes at the heart of this sense of ego, so much so that it often comes with a warning label from meditation teachers: Don't try this exercise unless you are prepared for where it might lead. The exercise is simple. Ask yourself the question, "Who am I?" Then, negate every answer.

I might answer, "I am John Cunyus." In response, my mind would point out that "John Cunyus" is just a sound. Well then, am I this physical person? This so-called physical person is an ongoing biological event that will one day end. Am I the thought-process behind it? Well, that thought-process too will end. And onward it goes.

Buddha insists there is nothing in reality corresponding to our notion of self. The notion of self is itself impermanent. This impermanence is the source of much of our dissatisfaction.
What possible benefit comes from reflecting on these three, unpleasant-seeming marks of existence? If we are content with life, then perhaps none. If we're not content, though, then the three marks can start us toward a deeper understanding.

At some point, mental health comes from being able to see life as it is, without fooling ourselves. Genuine life is found when we know our actual condition, not when we convince ourselves things aren't as they seem. We don't grow in life by running away from our situation as it is, but by changing our relationship with our real situation.

How does this happen? In Buddhism, it starts by understanding the role desire plays in the suffering that so often fills our days. We desire a world that doesn't change, at least when we are content. The fact that we don't live in such a world causes us to suffer. We desire a life that isn't full of dissatisfaction, at least on a material level. The fact that life isn't that way causes us to suffer. We desire a state where our sense of self is permanent, assured, unchanging. The fact that this never happens causes us to suffer.

Is it easier to change the outer reality of life or to gain control of the desire to have what we cannot have? Making life permanent, removing its dissatisfaction, even establishing an immovable sense of self, these things are beyond our ability. Yet if we understand this, clearly, we can change our attitude toward it.

Buddha challenges us to come to terms with our own desires. Wanting life to be something other than impermanent won't make it so. How will we relate to the impermanence around us?

It's easy to misunderstand the Buddhist answer to that question. For instance, I love my children more than life itself and want only blessing for them. Reality, however, is that they will suffer in life, regardless of my desire. Someday I will either lose them or they will lose me. Would I be better off not having children, then, since I know that pain is unavoidable?

At this point, I don't believe so. Nevertheless, I can imagine circumstances that might make me change my mind, not so much because of my pain but because of the pain my children might suffer. I have to learn how to love without blinders. I have to learn to love them as they are, not as I wish they were.

I have to learn to love without being attached to outcomes I can't control. Is it enough for me to love them fully in the present moment, doing the best I know how to do with and for them, fully understanding that sometimes things will go well and sometimes they won't? Can I love and then leave the outcome alone? Do I have to worry obsessively about matters beyond my control?

In this sense, the answer seems obvious. Wisdom points us back to this present moment as the only possible time to love our families, do meaningful work, and build meaningful relationships. And accepting life as it is, not as we wish it would be, makes building meaningful lives in the present moment more of a possibility, not less.

Life is impermanent. As we commonly live it, it is dissatisfying. Nothing in life corresponds to our customary idea of self. Coming to terms with this certainly undercuts one of society's primary ways of understanding. Yet it also frees us to love without illusions, to work without getting hung up on outcomes, to be fully and freely alive in the here and now.

Is it a brutal truth? Only experience can say.

****

A Willingness to Face Death

We live in a culture that worships physical beauty and worldly success. As such, it is hard for us to understand just how thoroughly the Buddhist method rejects those very things. Just as Buddhism cannot be understood without some sort of meditation practice, neither can it be understood without clearly seeing its rejection of physical beauty and earthly success.

The method uses graphic language to undermine our customary sense of physical beauty. Even an outwardly attractive person, we are reminded, is made up of:

> ... *nails, teeth, skin, flesh, sinews, bones, marrow of the bones, kidneys, heart, liver, pleura, spleen, lungs, intestines, mesentery, stomach, feces, bile, phlegm, pus, blood, sweat, fat, tears, lymph, saliva, snot, synovial fluid, urine, brain of the head."* (BIT, pg. 130)

When we consider the parts of the body separately, we find nothing attractive about them. Such aversion is something the method encourages us to develop. Just as the method reduces the seeming unity of the ego to the five skandhas, so does it reduce an attractive body to its constituent parts.

The monks are urged to meditate directly on death. As a passage from the Digha Nikaya Sutra states:

> *But again, O priests, a priest, if perchance he sees in a cemetery a decaying body one day dead, or two days dead, or three days dead, swollen, black, and full of festering putridity, he compares his own body, saying, 'Verily, my body also has this nature, this destiny, and is not exempt.'* (BIT, pg. 360-361)

Obviously, our methods of disposing of corpses have improved since Gautama's day. Most of us have never seen dead bodies in anything like the state the Sutra describes. We prefer to dress death up, put makeup on it, pretend it doesn't exist. It is to be ignored, denied, and overlooked. The Buddhist obsession with it seems beyond morbid to most of us. What possible purpose is served by being so frank about death?

As always, the method's purpose is to break us free of our illusions and attachments. Humanity "is captivated, entranced, spell-bound by its lusts." (BIT, pg. 336) It believes the things after which it lusts will bring it satisfaction, purpose, and meaning. The sad truth is that these things which we believe will bring us freedom actually end up enslaving us.

In focusing us unflinchingly on what physical life actually is, the method reminds us of the futility of spending our lives in pursuit of things that ultimately disappoint. It isn't that life is without meaning. In fact, the method sees life as precious. This life is our only opportunity to grasp the Ultimate, to taste *Nirvana*. It is our chance to find a peace that isn't dependent on things that pass away.

Before we can grasp the Ultimate, though, something must wake us up from the illusion that physical beauty and earthly success are what really matter. These reflections on the body and on death are radical therapy, designed to bring about such an awakening. Gautama describes the logic that drives him:

> *And being, O priests, myself subject to birth, I perceived the wretchedness of what is subject to birth.* (BIT, pg. 338)

The method's willingness to look directly at death seems odd, even grotesque, to us. Yet, if understood correctly, it opens our eyes to our genuine condition. It makes it possible for us to focus on what we truly are, rather than on what we wish we were. It helps us move beyond the suffering that keeps us in the grip of this fleeting world.

Indian Psychology

Asian Indian psychology, dating back at least to Gautama's day, imagines human beings as having at least six "energy centers," or *chakras*. Each of the six relates to a vital area of human life. We may or may not be conscious of all six at once. Still, conscious or not, all six centers influence at any given moment.

The lowest of the six centers has to do with physical survival. We take this for granted almost all the time. Yet when something threatens our physical life, we see immediately that this center is active and vital.

The next center has to do with desire. At its most basic, it concerns itself with reproducing the species. After that, its concern is pleasure. Most ads are pitched directly at this particular center. It is certainly alive and well in most of us.

The third center has to do with power. First of all, it's involved with establishing our own independence. Yet in some this longing for power overwhelms everything else. History is full of people with a seemingly limitless thirst for power.

The first three centers concern physical life and its trappings. For many, those aspects of life dominate everything. Aside from survival, pleasure, and power, what is there? Yet the ancient psychologists of India insisted that life had not really begun until the higher three centers awakened.

The fourth center, the one which begins the higher life, is the center of love. Once the center of love, of the heart, opens, life is transformed. To live a meaningful life, we need to reach the point of loving another selflessly. For me, this aspect of life began when I became a father. Others experience it differently. However we experience it, love is the great force which lifts us beyond ourselves.

The fifth center has to do with vision, our mental image of what life is. For many of us, life seems fixed, unchangeable. We accept patterns that were handed to us by our parents, who in turn accepted their parents' patterns, and so on. But our vision can change. In fact, genuine advances in human life almost always occur because someone refused to be limited by what already was. Instead, they had a vision of what could be.

Still, the Indian writers insisted that vision without love was dangerous. Without love, vision devolves into a power trip. Vision, guided by love, has the power to remake not just our own lives. Guided by The Ultimate, it can remake the world around us. Consider the vision of those who saw a world without slavery, for instance. This is the aspect of life Paul the Apostle likens to calling *"into existence the things that do not exist.*[6]" What is your vision?

The highest center of all concerns our relationship with the Ultimate. When this aspect of our lives opens, our communion with the Ultimate ceases to be a mere thought or a sentiment. It becomes central to all we are and do. This aspect of life corresponds to Jesus' words in John's gospel: *"Unless you are born again, you cannot see the kingdom of God.*[7]"

All these centers function in each of us, the Indians said. We alone choose where we place our effort. One key to mental health is learning to focus our energies where they matter most. Where are your energies focused now?

****

---

[6]Romans 4:17

[7]John 3:3

Ten Perfections of a Bodhisattva

The Asian Indian tradition believes in reincarnation. According to this belief, each of us has lived innumerable times in the past and will live innumerable times in the future. Though the different Indian religious traditions express the idea differently, the central belief in reincarnation is always similar. Some things, apparently, take more than one lifetime to master.

Siddhartha Gautama didn't decide one day he wanted to be a Buddha, nor was becoming a Buddha an accident. According to the tradition, Gautama vowed eons before to seek Buddha-hood, not for himself only but for the sake of all creatures.. Over the course of the lifetimes that followed, he perfected ten attributes consciously, in order to fully comprehend the Buddha nature.

In each successive lifetime, Gautama practiced, then mastered, the perfections. The perfections offer a behavioral guide to those working the Buddhist method. Consider each as it relates to your own life.

Generosity Gautama learned to be generous the way a fruit tree is generous. When a tree has fruit, anyone who wishes may come and take it. Its nature is to give, not to hold back.

Precepts   Buddhism has five precepts which are generally considered binding on all Buddhist, lay or monastic. Gautama shaped his existence according to the precepts in all circumstances[8].

Renunciation   Gautama renounced any and all sense of ownership, either of self or life or others.

Wisdom   Some knowledge is built in to the universe. Some principles are certain. More than mere knowledge, Wisdom understands and works with the flow of existence. Gautama sought complete wisdom through countless lifetimes.

Courage   This perfection, courage, is not rashness, as Aristotle said. No one is fearless. Courage is the willingness to face our fear, to fulfill our obligations. Gautama lived courageously, even in lives that to others seemed mundane.

Patience   Gautama learned to be patient, as the earth itself is patient. The earth does not respond in anger even to those who dump toxins into it. Neither did Gautama respond in anger.

Truth   Gautama learned to value that which corresponded to reality. Truth is more than a "head" thing. As the planets move according to the

---

[8] 1. Respect life. 2. Respect property. 3. Respect promises. 4. Respect words. 5. Respect the body.

truth of the gravitational force that holds them, so he learned to move in total obedience to truth.

Good Will Gautama practiced the same kindness to all persons, regardless of the other person's action. This, the ancient accounts note, is a costly perfection to master.

Determination Gautama mastered the art of intentional living. Through countless lifetimes, on all levels of consciousness, one goal was sought.

Indifference Gautama learned to respond to all actions without regard to their effect on him personally. Again, the story uses the analogy of the earth. The earth remains indifferent to its own gain, whether someone drops rose petals or human waste on it.

Few of us ever travel down the road of the perfections, certainly not to the road's end. Some of us never begin down the road at all, whether from ignorance or outright rejection.

The lesson of Buddhist experience, though, is that a life lived seeking the ten perfections is better able to deal with suffering and pain. Does it work?

The only way to find out is by practicing.

****

A Radical Negation

Original Buddhism was not for the faint of heart. Gautama and his closest followers renounced the world, abandoning ordinary routines of family, work, and society. They earned their living by begging and gave no thought to issues of social acceptance and worldly prosperity that preoccupy most of us in the course of our days. As an ongoing discipline, they limited themselves to one meal a day. Owning nothing more than a few robes and a bowl, the first Buddhists actively rejected much of what their neighbors considered indispensable.

Their method denied much of what their contemporaries and ours took for granted. Gautama insisted there was no ego, no self. He laid the blame for most of life's suffering on the very idea of an ego. Life was a curse, not a blessing, a sign of having fallen into ignorance and attachment. Birth, far from being something to celebrate, gave rise to the gravest afflictions: "*old age and death, sorrow, lamentation, misery, despair, and grief.*" As long as someone retained the slightest attachment to life, salvation was impossible.

Though ordinary people had a role to play in Buddhism, the method made clear that the real Buddhists were the monks, the ones who had given everything up to walk in Gautama's footsteps. Lay Buddhists supported the monks in their quest for

Nirvana. The laity, though, could not hope to attain *Nirvana* themselves in this lifetime. The best they could hope for was to earn merit enough to be reborn in a better place.

Needless to say, most of us aren't ready to abandon our families, homes, and jobs in order to seek *Nirvana*. If we are honest with ourselves, many of us find the Buddha's insistence that there is no self laughable. Of course there is a self, we say. If not, who did Buddha think he was teaching? Who, indeed, did the teaching to start with? Despite these obvious contradictions, the method still attracts hundreds of millions of people around the world. Many remain focused on this teaching that seems to fly in the face of everything we know. The reason begins where the Buddhist method itself does: with the reality of suffering.

We may not be ready to deny the reality of the ego or to reject all attachments to the world. We may be certain that some things are worth suffering for, worth remaining attached to. All of us, though, need ways of coping with the pain life carries with it.

We have a variety of ways of coping with that pain today. We can allow others to medicate it, assuming the medication is available and affordable to us. We can self-medicate through drugs and alcohol. We can try to work through it with counselors, ministers, and psychologists. We can attempt to bury it through our work, our religion, our family. All the evidence, though, suggests that these things aren't enough. The pain continues.

Buddhism offers a non-medical, non-chemical, non-ideological method for overcoming suffering. We don't have to be able to afford the treatments. We don't have to be religious in a particular way. Anyone who chooses to can meditate and put the dharma into practice. It does not belong only to those who use it to take themselves out of the world.

This, for me, is the central attraction. Gautama and the monks carried the method to its logical conclusion. They lived it fully and, in so doing, demonstrated its power to lead human beings to an abiding peace. To this day, Gautama's monks continue walking in his footsteps. The way of radical negation remains open. Those who cannot abandon the world, though, who remain bound to families, homes, jobs, and countries, are not left without hope, either. Unlike many religious or political positions, Buddhism is not an "all-or-nothing" proposition.

The method reminds us that, ultimately, there is no fixed, non-changing ego. Our identity, even in this life, changes. Who we are at age six is not who we are at age thirty-six or age sixty-six. When we forget this and cling fearfully to an identity we're afraid to lose, the method reminds us that both the identity and the fear are illusions. There is a truth that transcends them both.

When we see this, we see that the way of radical negation is open for us. We understand how some can leave the rat race behind, abandon the straitjacket of conventional life, and lose the fragile ego in the ocean of the Ultimate. We, too, under the right circumstances, could walk that path. Some days being a monk seems like an attractive alternative.

The path, though, is not one someone else can walk for us. For some, the call to the monastery is the only legitimate expression of the method. For others, though, it leads not away from society, but rather into its heart. Once we understand the method, we realize that its value is not so much in where we choose to live it out. Its value is in that we choose to live it out.

The method takes us to a place where there is no self, no ego, and no permanent identity. It empowers us to see things from that perspective. In relative terms, though, most of us retain our obligations, our bonds of love, our smaller self. We remain engaged with the world. The method helps us keep that engagement in perspective.

Those who have no sense of the Ultimate live and work in this world as if this world were the Ultimate. Then, when the things of this life change and slip away, they grieve the loss of the very things that give their life meaning. In meditation, though, using the method, we see that our identity in this world is a role, no more or less important than any other role someone may be playing. The role changes, but the Ultimate does not. This frees us to play the role before us, understanding it for what it is and not expecting it to be what it is not.

It is as if I am an actor, cast in the greatest role of my life. I play my part with such energy that I lose myself completely in it. My character's suffering is my suffering. My character's victories are my victories. My enthusiasm for the part makes it believable.

Sometimes we act our parts with such intensity we forget entirely that there is an existence off the stage. The events taking place on life's stage become so overwhelming that we cannot see beyond them. When the character we play dies, we believe we die as well.

Yet the play ends. Life's great drama is just that: a drama. When I am lost in the drama, the method reminds me who I am and, just as importantly, who I am not. Practicing the method, staying in touch with the Ultimate, I am grounded to play my part in life more effectively.

Many things become clearer as this happens. I understand better how pain and fear drive my decisions, for instance. I learn I don't have to fear what happens on the stage. I remember this is a role I am playing, not the whole of reality. I become a more effective human being because I am less driven by fear.

Yet the insight doesn't stop there. I don't just see the way pain and fear have shaped my actions. I begin to see other peoples' actions differently as well. I understand that they are playing a role, too, even if they don't understand it themselves. Others have trouble seeing beyond the drama onstage, just like me. Others struggle with the pain and fear of losing what they believe themselves to be. When I understand that, I can live with greater compassion.

While I am trapped in my role onstage, I can't help feeling threatened by what happens there. I judge everything else in my little world by whether I believe it makes things better or worse for me in my little role. Once I see that I am not threatened by what happens on stage, that my deepest identity lies beyond it, my anxiety eases. Though others act out of pain and fear, I do not have to. And, when circumstances permit, I can use this insight to help them see beyond their pain as well.

The method is, indeed, a radical negation of a life lived trapped on stage. Following it to its logical conclusions does indeed place us beyond the boundaries of the drama. It doesn't compel us to leave the drama, though. It frees us to choose the manner in which we will play our part. Buddhism's radical negation does not make us less human. If anything, when we practice it, it makes us more human, wherever we end up playing our role in the great drama of life.

****

Why Do Bad Things Happen, Period

Sooner or later, every human being encounters sorrow, suffering, and loss. Sooner or later, the things each human being values will be tested by sorrow, suffering, and loss, as well. When we suffer, we find out quickly that some things are worth the pain and many others are not. Each religious tradition must offer an answer to the question of why bad things happen to good people. In fact, each must answer the deeper question of why bad things happen at all, regardless of to whom they happen.

This question seems more problematic for theistic traditions, ones that believe in a personal God. If a good, all-powerful being created the world, why does that being allow innocent suffering? Most of us have less of a problem with the suffering of those we consider bad people. We understand, usually in the abstract, that sinners get punished. But when people who aren't bad in our eyes suffer, we wonder where a good, all-powerful God is in the process. What did the children of Iraq do to deserve the torments so many have suffered?

When we suffer personally, the question becomes even more difficult. Surely we aren't "bad people!" We may be misunderstood. We may have made mistakes. But do we deserve cancer, for instance?

Is it right that we or our loved ones should die in pain while others seem to get off scot free?

If God exists, if God is good, and if God is all-powerful, why do such things happen? Why couldn't God create a world in which suffering wasn't necessary? Why can't God step in and stop suffering, at least when it involves innocent children (or us!). Is God unable to stop it? Do we all deserve suffering, however innocent we may seem?

There are several schools of thought on the subject. Certain passages in the Bible explicitly connect suffering with sin. Those who do evil suffer for it. Yet the Bible itself understands that this teaching doesn't fit all circumstances. In the Book of Job, Job's friends argue that he suffers because he has sinned. Job insists that isn't the case. Ultimately, God appears and eases Job's pain, without answering Job's questions.

Some argue that suffering has a redemptive value. Biblical texts, like the Suffering Servant passages of Isaiah or the stories of Christ's passion, point this direction. Many people through the course of human history have endured terrible sorrow, eased by the hope that a larger purpose is being served. Though this answer offers comfort, it leaves unanswered the question of why a loving, almighty Being permits it to start with.

For some, the question itself is blasphemous. Once, in the throes of a clinical depression, I asked a conservative Christian preacher, "If God is so good, why does life hurt so bad?" He responded by telling me I was "just a heartbeat away from eternal separation from God" and needed to repent of asking such questions. In this view, we are to trust God and stifle our doubts.

For others, the question has no answer. Life has no larger purpose, no redemptive value. We are thrown into suffering, ready or not. To ask for fairness in such a circumstance is absurd.

Buddha begins answering the question by reminding us what is not going on here. The process is not aimed at us, personally. We are not separate, permanent individuals who suffer either justly or unjustly. The illusion that we are only makes the suffering worse. Suffering, Buddha teaches, is neither just nor unjust. Suffering is simply the nature of existence.

****

To illustrate this, Gautama taught what has become known as "The Wheel of Existence":

> *From uncertainty, change arises;*
> *From change, consciousness arises;*
> *From consciousness,*

> *name and form arise;*
> *From name and form,*
> *the six organs of sense arise;*
> *From the six organs of sense,*
> *contact arises;*
> *From contact, sensation arises;*
> *From sensation, desire arises;*
> *From desire, attachment arises;*
> *From attachment, existence arises;*
> *From existence, birth arises;*
> *From birth,*
> *old age and death,*
> *sorrow, lamentation, misery,*
> *grief, and despair arise.*
>
> *Thus this entire aggregation of misery arises.*

The immediate cause of our suffering, he states, is birth. Birth is the way living beings come into existence, just as death is the way they leave it. Because we have been born, we are subject "old age and death, sorrow, lamentation, misery, grief, and despair."

Obvious as this is, it is a truth many of us overlook. While sometimes we do suffer for the wrongs we have done, far more often we suffer simply because we live in a body. Our bodies are subject to illness, injury, defect, and death. No amount of wishful thinking can change that.

Despite that, many of us somehow expect a life that has only pleasure, not pain. It still shocks us when we or those we love suffer. When suffering happens, we tend to look around for someone or something to blame. Believing ourselves to be personal beings, we can't help but take suffering personally. To help us beyond that, Buddha patiently carries us back beyond the curtain, to see where suffering arises.

If suffering arises from birth, birth arises from existence. Existence, Buddha teaches, arises from attachment. We are attached to staying alive, at the most basic level. When we stay alive for awhile, we get attached to other things: food, clothing, and shelter among them. As our existence becomes more secure, we are able to attach ourselves to ever higher desires, as described in Abraham Mazlow's "Hierarchy of Needs.". Those who are starving don't worry about looking for sex, after all. Attachment, though, is neither good nor bad, in and of itself.

Whatever else living beings may be attached to, we are almost always attached to pleasure. We seek what feels good to us, not what feels bad. I prefer pleasure to pain. I seek pleasurable experiences. The sex act is pleasurable. My attachment to pleasure, the fact that I seek it above most things, has led directly to the births now of four children.

Birth, as I know, leads to the suffering we experience.

Attachment arises from desire. When something satisfies a desire in a pleasant manner, we want more of it. Desire arises from sensation. If we don't itch, we don't scratch. When we itch, we experience a sensation leading to a desire in the same instance.

Sensation arises from contact. We come into contact with something and, obviously, we feel it. No contact, no feeling.

We come into contact with the things through our senses: taste, smell, touch, sight, sound, and imagination. Without the senses, touch would lead to no sense of contact.

We have senses because there is something out there to sense. This Buddhists call this something name and form. We recognize name and form in the world out there because we are conscious.

Consciousness comes from the fact that the universe changes. The universe has a specific character. It has an almost limitless number of future possibilities, but what it has been is already formed. Change is neither moral nor immoral. Change happens because there is uncertainty at the heart of things.

Uncertainty is an emptiness at the heart of things, a primal dissatisfaction with the way things are. This discomfort drives that which is to seek that which is not. It compels all things to seek that which they do not possess. This, in turn, moves the whole mechanism from the moment of birth to the present. The question of why we suffer leads us across the whole gamut of existence.

The Buddhist method shows us both why and how suffering comes about. Once we realize it, we can choose at least a bit more consciously what desires we give in to, for instance, or what attachments we can let go. Most of us, though, want more.

We want to know who is responsible for suffering. Was it something we did? Is it something God does to us? People wanted to know such things in Gautama's day, too.

He addressed the question repeatedly. First of all, the question itself is not correct. If I say, 'I suffer,' this implies belief in an 'I' that suffers. Does this 'I' continue after death, or does it end, Gautama was often asked.

Instead of saying 'The ego continues' or, 'The ego doesn't continue,' Gautama pointed to a deeper truth. The 'I' whose fate we are discussing is an idea, not a being. Nothing in the process, no permanent entity, corresponds to this 'I'.

To address suffering, Gautama says, address the 'I' first. Get beyond seeing this process as something personal, directed either for, by, or against you. When we practice this way, suffering shows itself in a different light.

It isn't that suffering goes away for those who use the Buddhist method. It is that it ceases to be personal.

The method leads us to renounce the entire idea of ourselves as permanent entities. It meditates on the reality of the non-personal processes that constitute the world. Just as the earth does not flinch, whether we piss on it or pour out sweet tea, so we become indifferent to the effect of change on our egos.

The method offers a perspective from which we see all that is, ourselves included, without unnecessary attachment. This implies a different way of seeing ourselves, others, and the world, a way that at first seems alien and forbidding.

The point, though, is that Buddhism is a method. It isn't a matter of believing it once and living happily ever after. It is a discipline one puts into practice on a daily basis.

Only then will we be in a position to judge for ourselves whether this answer to suffering is valid or not.

Salvation in the Asian Indian Tradition

Salvation means different things to people from different parts of the world. To understand why, we need to know what people assume they are being saved from. For someone in the Asian Indian tradition, salvation means escaping from the endless cycle of birth and death. For a traditional monotheist, Jew, Christian, or Muslim, salvation means salvation from sin and death.

The differences in how each understands salvation grow out of the way each conceives of the significance of our present lives. To a traditional Christian, individual life is unique, precious, created by God. Time is finite in the Christian imagination as well. The universe of the biblical accounts is scarcely more than six thousand years old. Things have not had time to get old and wear out. This unique life is threatened by sin, which devalues life, and damnation, which is eternal separation from God.

Those in the Indian tradition see it differently. Life is something mind-bogglingly old, stretching out almost infinitely from an unimaginable beginning. Death doesn't end things in the least. The concept of reincarnation means individual souls cannot escape not only dying, but being born.

Through unimaginable stretches of time, we have been born, lived, died, forgotten, and been born again. Progress is an illusion. What goes up, must come down. Life travels in endless spirals, tracing a path that, while never completely the same, always disappoints us in familiar ways. Heaven, that fond vision of Western theists, does not last forever. One eventually falls from such happiness into darker realms.

The problem for a Hindu or Buddhist is not being born again, in the Christian sense. It isn't that the peoples of the East didn't believe in heaven. The universe abounds with heavens, as many as the stars above. It is full of hells, too. None of them, however, lasts forever.

Even if heaven lasts a million years, it seems of no consequence ultimately once it is gone. The gods themselves die and are reborn. In the great, endless, brutal sweep of evolutionary change, no eternal salvation is possible within the <u>wheel of existence</u>. Birth, death, and rebirth are a cycle no one escapes.

Salvation, in this tradition, is letting go of the cycle. For the Hindu, it is *moksha*, liberation in Sanskrit, release from the necessity of birth and death. For a Buddhist, it is *Nirvana*, as we have previously discussed.

A Hindu conceives salvation as a merging into the ocean of the divine being, losing our narrow, little self in the endlessness of God. Buddhists imagine a state where, in the words of The Heart Sutra, *"There is no form, no eye, no ear, no nose, no tongue, no body, and no mind."*

Both monotheists and Indians believe in salvation, however differently they conceive it. Both agree that salvation is, to some degree, a present reality. Both share a concern for morality. Both encourage a disciplined life of faith, one that is a matter not of words only but of deeds.

Common ground exists among religious traditions on many levels. Many different traditions produce individuals who live genuinely saintly lives. Humanity's heroes of spirit come in both genders and in all colors.

Our human nature leads all of us down a path marked by suffering and hardship. No one escapes, whatever their religion, nationality, or economic status. Nothing in our physical world lasts forever, however long some things seem to last.

We have a common human ground and share a common human yearning for salvation, however differently we understand it. Isn't the next step in moral development learning to empathize with each other in our struggles and help each other toward that deepest longing?

****

God in Buddhism

Those of us raised in Western, God-centered faiths like Judaism and Christianity naturally wonder, if and when we consider Buddhism, what Buddhism teaches about God. Do Buddhists believe in God? Is Buddha himself a God? What role does God play in Buddhism?

First of all, Gautama did not see himself as a god. He was a human, like every other human. He never taught his followers to worship him. He stressed throughout his life that the teaching was what mattered. When he died, the teaching endured, not the human being.

Buddha taught that arguments over God's existence or non-existence "tend not to enlightenment." Buddha described arguments over such topics God as

> "*a jungle, a wilderness, a puppet show, a writhing, and a fetter, and is coupled with misery, ruin, despair, and agony* " (BIT, pg. 125).

Arguing about God does not help us deal with the real problem of life: suffering.

The universe, for Gautama, was not a pleasant place. It was a slaughter-house, a place where life feeds on life, where the vain round of birth, suffering, loss, and death stretches on without end. Why speculate about who is responsible for such a situation?

Our deepest need, rather, is to acknowledge suffering, understand its origin and cessation, and walk the path that leads to suffering's extinction. When asked abstract questions, like that concerning the existence of God, Gautama responded by directing the questioner back to what is here and now, back to the task at hand.

Gautama seems to have accepted the existence of the Hindu gods. Those deities played a role in the stories his followers told of his life. Yet he considered that the gods were trapped inside the same cycle of birth and death that ensnared everything else in existence.

For all their present happiness, the gods were in a worse condition when it came to overcoming suffering than humans. The gods' happiness blinds them to their own reality. Because they were comfortable and happy, blessed with long and pleasant lives, they had trouble understanding that they, too, were destined to die. They, too, would one day fall from their exalted position and be reborn in lesser circumstances. (In that sense, the gods seem like modern citizens of the West, prosperous in the midst of global poverty.)

Humans alone had a chance of grasping the truth that led beyond suffering. Humans shared a measure of the gods' intelligence, yet did so within a frailer body, one prone to disease, hardship, and sorrow. It is our very human weakness that opens us to the teaching that does away with suffering.

The lesson is obvious. Let's not get bogged down in questions that don't help us. Let's instead focus on a truth that makes this life more livable for all concerned.

****

What in Tarnation Is Reincarnation?

The English word "reincarnation" derives from the ancient Greek word *carne*, meaning "body" or flesh. Reincarnation expresses the belief that a spark of divinity within each living thing can neither die nor be born. This spark, known in different traditions by a variety of names, incarnates, literally takes on flesh, over and over again. It animates a physical body, yet has its root in a dimension transcending our conscious awareness.

We live our individual lives believing ourselves to be unique. In fact, we are unique as individuals, yet that uniqueness only extends to a certain degree. The individual existence is transient, fleeting. It cannot be held. As Paul the Apostle said, "*Flesh and blood cannot inherit the kingdom of God.*[9]"

Past a certain point, there is only Spirit. Spirit, by definition, cannot be defined completely (nice little logical trap, huh). Spirit is a Mystery to our conscious awareness. Spirit is that by which we live and move and have our being. Yet, in the same way the eye cannot see itself or the fingertip touch itself, we cannot capture the Spirit which makes us.

---

[9] 1 Corinthians 15:50

Spirit, the Ultimate, can be approached indirectly, though. We can calm ourselves into an awareness of it. Yet we can neither grasp it nor lose it.

For those in the Hindu/Buddhist traditions, the fact that we are born, live, and die over and over again is not something to be celebrated. This round of rebirth, called *samsara* in Sanskrit, is a prison of suffering, rooted in ignorance of who we truly are. There are a variety of paths to escape the wheel of death in life, yet all ultimately lead to the same, transcendent destination.

Some say, naturally enough, "If we have lived again and again and again, why don't we remember those past lives?" According to the Hindu/Buddhist tradition, memories of the past life are extinguished for most at the moment of birth, thus conditioning the individual to repeat the life cycle again. In Greek mythology, the souls of the dead in Hades drank from the River *Lethe*, "forgetfulness," prior to being reborn.

Nevertheless, the Hindu/Buddhist metaphysicians insist we inherit the tendencies of all our past lives. Whether we call that process reincarnation, as Hindus do, transmigration, or genetic inheritance, the phenomenon is widely described by both religious and scientific observers.

God, the Ultimate Reality at the heart of existence, does not suffer through individual incarnations with us except at moments of God's own choosing. God abides in what the Hindus call *sat, chit, ananda,* "being, consciousness, bliss," at the root of all phenomenal existence.

In meditation, in worship, and in consecrated action, individuals on the wheel of rebirth can taste the "being, consciousness, bliss" of divinity. Such tastes lead beyond themselves, ultimately to the goal of most Asian religious thought: liberation from the necessity of birth and death. To attain the goal, it isn't necessary for us to abandon our lives as they are. In fact, fulfilling one's responsibilities to self, family, and society is indispensable in Hindu thought.

What we must overcome is our attachment to those things. We must see beyond the illusion that the only reality is the one experienced through our senses. We must patiently await the moment when the divine reality within us and at the heart of all things dawns on our consciousness.

****

****

> "Blunt the sharpness,
> Untangle the knot,
> Soften the glare,
> Merge with the dust."
>
> --*Tao Te Ching, Book IV*

****

Applications

Five Steps to a Happier Life

1. Manage expectations. Most of us expect the world to be different than it is. We expect it, somehow, to conform to our desires. We get upset when the world isn't the way we want, often without ever accepting that it is what it is. Saying the world is what it is doesn't mean we have to be passive. Our freedom to act is part of the world being the way it is. Still, most of us allow ourselves to be bothered by things that are way beyond our control.

Ask, 'What are my expectations?'

2. Listen to your body. I had migraines for years and tried many medicines. Only gradually did it occur to me that the problem wasn't entirely with my body. The problem was with the stressful circumstances in which I found myself. My body was trying to tell me to find a different way. When I began listening to my body, the headaches began to diminish. What are your physical symptoms telling you?

Ask, 'What is my body telling me?'

3. Do what is before you to do, then let it go. We get hung up on outcomes. As youngsters, we go through periods of great self-consciousness, worried about what others think of us. We believe that, if only we can make certain things happen, other people will feel good about us. As we age, hopefully we grow beyond such self-consciousness. Each of us has won a few, lost a few, and tied some others. Sometimes we win, sometimes we don't. A happier course is to find something we love to do, then do it. Do it not so others will feel better about us, but because we love to do it. If we succeed, we succeed. If not, then not. When we work because we enjoy what we're doing, the outcome doesn't matter as much.

Ask, 'What is my task at this moment?'

Ask, 'What can I now let go of?'

4. Remember what you are. You are an animate body, aware of itself, partly conscious and partly not. You are a series of thoughts, emotions, memories, and sensations. Your feelings come and go like clouds in the sky. You can't hold them, even when you want to. Remember what you are, and, conversely, what you aren't. If there is a Self in you, something that knows the thoughts, the body, the emotions, and all, this Self probably isn't what you thought it was. Take time to get to know what you really are.

Ask, 'What am I?'

5. Understand and forgive. I know I've made bad decisions when I act out of fear. I have come to regret many of those decisions, as I suppose all of us do. Others also make poor decisions out of fear. I need to understand that, to understand that most of us are doing the best we can with what we have. Understanding my own weaknesses helps me understand why others sometimes act in ways that hurt. They aren't any more (or less) malicious than me. This helps us not take things too personally, to be more tolerant when there is pain. Understanding myself makes it possible for me to forgive. It makes it possible not only for me to forgive others, but for me to forgive myself.

Ask, 'Who do I need to forgive?

****

Five Ways Our Thoughts Can Make Us Sick

The human mind is a wondrous organ. It regulates the functioning of this entire incredibly complex body of ours. At the same time, it allows us to carry on our ordinary lives, taking care of the business below our conscious awareness.

Conscious awareness is a one-pointed affair, for most folks. That means we are able to deal with one issue, one topic, at a time. Because mind moves swiftly, this is seldom a limitation to us. Mind fills in the gaps for us.

Sometimes, though, our conscious awareness becomes so full, so clogged, that we tune out everything else. When we become consciously unaware of issues on the psychological level, mind continues to process them.

Normally, in a low stress, low distraction, environment, we would deal with such inner concerns in a more conscious fashion. Unfortunately, few of us live in low stress, low distraction environments. The mind has to get our conscious attention to get us to deal with the problems.

Here again we run into a glitch. Mind speaks the language of image and intuition. Reason and logic are functions of conscious mind, after all. Many of us are woefully out of tune with the language of image and intuition, at least as spoken to us by the mind.

When things get far enough out of whack, mind can communicate with us through symptoms of bodily discomfort. It's as if mind says, 'You won't listen to your own discomfort about that relationship? Alright, I'll send you a headache to make your time together even more uncomfortable.'
At times, it is as if mind is screaming to us, 'Get me outta here!'

How do we listen more effectively?

We listen more effectively to these inner intuitions by paying closer attention to the content of our thoughts. Are our thoughts negative, condemning, fearful? These emotions, unchecked, have a demonstrable negative effect on our health.

In fact, according to clinical psychologist Leslie LeCron, 80 to 85 percent of what we consider normal, physiological symptoms, are not organic at all. They aren't caused by something wrong with our bodies. They are caused by stress, by unresolved psychological tensions.

Here are five ways in which thoughts and emotions can make us sick.

Example
We find ourselves reacting to problems the same way important figures in our lives did. They got stress headaches, and so do we. Are you following someone else's example?

Suggestion
Suggestion is similar to Example, but more immediate. Why is it that many times we don't catch cold unless someone around us catches it first? Germs that cause such illnesses are often around us anyway. Our immune systems take care of most.

But under certain circumstances, like presence of someone else demonstrating symptoms, we become sick ourselves?
Suggestion, of course, isn't always the cause of our discomfort. Sometimes we actually catch contagious viruses and get sick. But suggestion plays a larger part than most of us suspect.

Conflict
Unresolved conflict, either external or internal, often manifests as a physical symptom. We get a migraine, for instance, or an upset stomach. While we can and often should medicate the symptom, unless we address the conflict that causes it we've only given ourselves a band-aid.

Most of us find conflict much more exhausting than we realize. It takes a far larger toll than we admit. Perhaps if we were more aware of its cost, we would involve ourselves in less of it.

Punishment

Let's face it. Sometimes we get away with things in the world that we know are wrong. Sometimes there is even a rush of satisfaction in doing so. But the nagging voice of conscience doesn't cease to speak. It speaks to us of, as Thomas Jefferson put it, "decent regard for the opinions of mankind."

If it can't get our attention consciously, it will be sure to get our attention through symptoms. The ancient Greeks told stories about the Furies, fierce beings who invisibly pursued hidden criminals and deviants. Eventually, unless we resolve the issue, those "furies" catch up to us. We unconsciously punish ourselves for the wrong we have done.

Unfortunately, we may punish ourselves long after the deed is done. Or we may get so in the habit of punishing ourselves that we do it continually, whether warranted or not.

The symptom can often be allayed by disciplines such as forgiveness, introspection, and focused awareness on the problem. Until we learn to recognize the symptom as what it is, though, we continue to suffer.

Avoidance

Some situations in life are far more uncomfortable for us than they seem on the surface. Perhaps we grew up in a difficult household. People pretended to be one thing when others were looking, but were someone else entirely in the home. It stressed us out hugely when we were kids, but we never called the stress by name. We were supposed to only say and think good things about family.

Then we went out into the world and discovered that it all wasn't like our family. That may have been a huge relief to us.
We may be living an entirely different way than our family of origin. But the "original sin," if you will, of our family remains unaddressed.

Every time we go to family engagements we get sick. We have headaches. We can't sleep. In some, small way at least, our bodies make us miserable while we are there.

We attribute it to the travel, the strange food, the change in routine. And while it may in fact have some relation to those things, it has a far larger relation to our mind's desire to avoid being there in the first place.

Our symptoms may arise because we are silently dreading something, but not admitting it to ourselves. Sometimes conscious mind plows ahead despite the pain. Sometimes that is the right thing to do.

Sometimes, though, it isn't. Sometimes we need to give ourselves room to come to terms with why we want to avoid the situation. Sometimes the body is exactly right: we can and should stay away, because no real good is gained by our suffering.

These are five ways our thoughts can make us sick:

1. Example.
2. Suggestion.
3. Conflict.
4. Punishment.
5. Avoidance.

Even Gandhi Had Karma

> "…he does not know the fruition of meritorious karma to be the misery it really is, seeing that it is completely overwhelmed with the calamities of birth, old age, disease, death, etc." (BIT, pg. 181)

Forgiveness, so we've been told, is a spiritual exercise. It's hard to get it if you don't give it, as Jesus himself pointed out. Yet forgiveness can be overdone.

We use it like a magic word, as if just saying "Forgive" makes everything better. It doesn't, necessarily. Forgiveness can't erase consequences. The law of karma isn't annulled by our forgiveness . . . or lack thereof.

Many have pointed out that repenting of something without turning away from it does little good. It seems to me that we often place more value on what our act of forgiveness should mean than reality does. Is it that we want someone to set us free from the consequences of what we do?

That's something no one can do. We unavoidably reap what we sow, "we" being the collective life on this planet. We may not see the full cycle of consequences acted out individually. We die too rapidly for that. Have no doubt about it, though. Life on the planet cannot escape the consequences of our actions.

Before we get to the subject of forgiveness, we need to come to terms with the law of karma. Karma is the sum total of all the actions by all the actors who have ever and will ever live (nice, small concept, ain't it!). Nothing shields us from karma, since we ourselves are products of karma.

Are we at peace with our actions in the world? By all means change them, if we aren't. If we're not, though, why not? By all means take stock.

Even Gandhi had karma, after all. Had there been no Gandhi, would there have been the collective Hindu-Muslim genocide of India's independence and all that followed? Millions died who most assuredly would not have died in that manner had the British remained as rulers. This does not take away from Gandhi's example. It only serves to show that all actions have consequences, whether we consider the actions good or not.

Am I at peace with my karma, my actions in the world? If I'm not, how can I be? What would it take for me to get there? How can I live proactively, to avoid actions I would rather not take?

"Would that even today you knew the things that make for peace! But now they are hid from your eyes,[10]" Jesus lamented over Jerusalem sometime around the year 30 AD. We're still asking the same question. What is needed for peace? Here is one way.

Forgive all you want, but live in such a way that further forgiveness is not necessary. Make peace with yourself, your world, your actions, and their consequences. Make peace, if necessary, with the idea that your actions don't mean much in the vastness of this universe. Make peace with not knowing the answer to every question. Make peace with sometimes not even having sense enough to ask a question.

Making peace happens by living peacefully. How can tormented souls make peace, when they haven't experienced it themselves? The Biblical admonition, *"Seek peace and pursue it[11]"* seems as valid as ever.

---

[10] Luke 19:42

[11] Psalm 34:14

Death on the Wheel of Existence

A dear friend of mine died of cancer recently. He was the kind of friend who stands by you when times are tough. He always had a smile on his face and brought a smile to mine. His family reflects him, too.

I know how hard losing a loved one is. I've been through it personally and been with others through it probably about five hundred times now, as a minister. I've seen sadness and loss.

Let's examine my friend's passing, in light of the Wheel of Existence.

Why did my friend die? Was it something he deserved? Was God punishing him for sin? Was there a transcendent meaning to his suffering? Was his suffering meaningless?

In the simplest terms, he died because he had been born. Birth is 100% fatal, given enough time. This is the fundamental reason for his suffering.

He was born because his parents existed. They continued existing because they were attached to various things in their life: among them, their own lives, each other (at least long enough to give birth to my friend), family, and friends.

They desired the things they were attached to. They found meaning in them. The things they enjoyed sustained them through good times and bad. It is well to desire such things.

They felt desire because they felt sensations. They preferred good sensations to indifferent or painful ones. Again, that is no surprise. We all prefer something that feels good, rather than something that feels bad.

They felt sensations because they had contact with different things. They had contact through their senses: sight, sound, touch, taste, smell, and imagination.

Those senses existed because there was a world outside of them. They knew the world outside them because they were conscious.

They were conscious of the outside world because it changed constantly. Where there is no change, there is no need for consciousness.

It changed constantly because there is uncertainty at its core.

Why such uncertainty exists, no one knows. When this whole process began, we can only guess, not having been there ourselves.

The point of all this is that the reason my friend died was because he had been born. The only way to avoid death is to avoid birth.

None of us had a choice when it came to being born. I don't remember asking for it, do you? Neither do we have a choice when it comes to dying.

Gautama believed he had lived countless lives in the past. According to the Buddhist scriptures, he could remember each of those lives clearly. He spoke about them in his teaching as casually as we would speak about our own memories of past events.

For Gautama, life as we normally live it had no redeeming characteristics. He had been born, lived, suffered, and died too many times to harbor hopes about anything in the physical world outside him.

Nirvana, total extinction, was his purpose. I understand and respect that, of course. I know my children are the dance of skandhas. They are as frail and fallible as me, yet I love them. I know full well what will happen to them, in the end.

They will die, as will I. We won't die because we've done anything in particular wrong or because we deserve it in a moral sense. We will die because we were born.

In the interim, while there is life, I will love and enjoy them as well as I am able. I will remind myself of what they (and I) are: flesh and blood, *carne y hueso*. I'll remind myself we are not permanent beings.

We and everything about us will come to an end, sometime in the not too distant future. Yet while I have life, I will love them. I will not abandon them until I must.

Gautama's method helps me keep my balance. It allows me to understand suffering in a non-personal way. His method allows me see clearly what's at stake in this world and what isn't.

Some of what's at stake is worth suffering for. I choose to suffer for some things. The method reminds me it is a choice.

Other suffering comes as a matter of course. It isn't personal.

So be it.

****

How to Use the Skandhas for Peace of Mind

See, "The Five Skandhas" for review.

We can use the teaching on the skandhas to defuse difficult emotional states. Instead of being overwhelmed by a troublesome event or memory, try breaking it down into its parts, using the method as a guide.

Let's say something painful happens to me at work. All too often, I carry that pain with me, letting it fester inside and cause even more misery. Surely there is a better way.

Here's how it can work.

1. I ask, 'What is the form of this situation?'
Form can be physical or mental, something happening right now or a memory. In this case, the event has already taken place. The form involved a memory of what happened. My pain was not being caused by a physical event in the present.

2. I ask, 'What is the sensation in this situation?'
The sensation is a mixture of pain, regret, and loss. If the sensation weren't difficult for me, I wouldn't have a problem. Still, we can too quickly label our sensations without truly feeling them.

3. I ask, 'What is the preference in this situation?'

We don't prefer pain, simply put. I react against a complicated sensation instinctively, trying to wipe it away. I acknowledge the preference, knowing that it is neither good nor bad in itself. Once the preference is conscious, though, I can choose differently if I need to.

4. I ask, 'What is the conditioning in this situation?'

I am conditioned to react against difficult emotions, without thought. That conditioning kicks in here as well. At this point, though, I can ask myself if I have to respond this way. Perhaps I can respond differently, once I become aware of what is going on.

5. I ask, 'What is the consciousness in this situation?'

Consciousness is a sequence of thoughts, emotions, and experiences, from which the idea of myself as an ongoing ego arises. If the sensations, preferences, and conditioning in the situation are unpleasant, they affect my "ego" in a negative way. My idea of self suffers. I stop and ask myself, though, what is really at risk. Usually, less is at risk than my conditioning led me to believe.

As a cumulative effect of the exercise, the emotions, the hurt, the pain tend to subside. I maintain a sense of balance through the difficulty, not giving way to the destructive energies. I resist the temptation to identify myself with the content of the skandhas, choosing to stay rooted in a deeper, more peaceful level of awareness.

****

The Anger-Eating Demon

Thus have I heard . . .

On one occasion, a sickly, spindly demon snuck past Indra's courtiers and sat down on his throne. Indra just so happened to be king of the gods at that moment.

Indra's court was not too happy about it. They shouted to each other and began to gather in the throne room to toss the demon back where it belonged . . . definitely out of Indra's throne.

After all, only Indra was allowed to sit there.

Each time they shouted, though, the sickly, spindly demon got a little healthier. At first this infuriated Indra's courtiers, so they began shouting louder. With each shout, the demon became larger, more menacing, and finally even fierce.

By the time Indra himself heard the commotion and came home, his courtiers were genuinely afraid of the monster who now sat on the king's throne. The words tumbled out of their panic as they reported to the king all that had happened. To their surprise Indra shushed them, commanding them to take a deep breath and "chill."

When all were silent, he entered the throne room
and stood respectfully before the monster
sitting there. "Peace to you, O anger-eating
demon," Indra said.

The courtiers were astonished. As they watched,
Indra, the king of the Gods, the universe's fiercest
warrior, bowed to a demon sitting on his throne.
No lightning bolts. No battle.

To their equal astonishment, the anger-eating
demon shrank visibly at the sound of Indra's words.

Indra repeated them. "Peace to you, O anger-eating
demon."

After several repetitions the demon vanished
entirely, never to be seen again.

    "Peace to you, O anger-eating demon."

****

Miscellaneous

Bibliography

Buddhism: In Translations, Henry Clarke Warren, translator, Cosimo Classics, New York, NY, 2005.

Buddhism: Its Essence and Development, Edward Conze, Harper Torchbooks, New York, 1975.

The Dhammapada, Juan Mascaro, tr, Penguin Classics, New York, 1973.

Holy Bible: New Revised Standard Version, National Council of the Churches of Christ, New York, 1989.

The Tao Te Ching, Lao Tsu, Gia Fu Feng and Jane English, translators, Vintage Books, New York, 1972.

The Relaxation Response, Herbert Benson and Miriam Zipper, William Morrow, New York, 1975.

About the Author

John Cunyus spent twenty years in the ordained ministry of the Christian Church (Disciples of Christ), serving churches in Pilot Point, Weatherford, Houston (twice), Lake Jackson, and Dallas, all in Texas.

Since leaving local church ministry in 2005, John has been publishing the website, .JohnCunyus.com, as well as a blog, "Rolling the Wheel." A sixth-generation Texan, Cunyus is a graduate of Rice, TCU, and Pacific Western Universities.

He is the author of eleven books, and is currently working on a translation of the Latin Old Testament.

Also by the Author
- Partners in Prayer, Chalice Press, 1992.
- Is It True? Examining the Core of Christian Faith, Searchlight Press, 1994.
- A Spiritual Assessment Inventory, UMI, 1996 (dissertation).
- Handmade Christians in a Cookie Cutter World, Chalice Press, 1997.
- Soulmapping: Exploring Your Inner Reality, Searchlight Press, 1998.
- *Disciples of Christ: Past and Future*, www.JohnCunyus.com, 2002.

- A Handbook for Christian Healing, Self-Published, 2002.
- Flames in the Jungle, iUniverse, 2006.
- Flames of Faith: A Thumbnail Guide to World Religions, iUniverse, 2006.
- Toromillo the Hunted, iUniverse, 2007
- The Way of Wisdom: Job, Proverbs, Ecclesiastes, Song of Solomon, Searchlight Press, 2008.

Special Thanks:

George M. Cunyus
Mary Jean Miles
Bruce and Patti Cunyus
Russell and Lisa Church
Suzie and Wendell Patterson
Jim and Carol Archer
Myles Hall
Norman Stolpe
Anonymous

Readers Say:

"You are applying Buddha's teachings to your own way. That can help those who are still wrestling with words and phrases. I like the way you adapted the dharma to modern day thought, and to your own personal experiences. A very good read and it makes for a refreshing perspective on a time-honored tradition.
– Rev. Yao Feng Shakya,
Buddhist Minister,
Eugene, Oregon

The Middle Way [the Buddhist method] provides a balance, incorporating asceticism and mysticism into a healthy approach to solving the problem of suffering, without a requirement that the Christian adopt beliefs or practices that are inconsistent with a personal relationship with Jesus Christ and a life led according to the Biblical principles.
– Myles Hall,
Christian Layperson,
Azle, Texas

****

> In emptiness,
> there is no form,
> no eye,
> no ear,
> no nose,
> no tongue,
> no body,
> no mind.
>
> -- *The Heart Sutra*

****

www.ingramcontent.com/pod-product-compliance
Lightning Source LLC
Chambersburg PA
CBHW070457100426
42743CB00010B/1657